PRAISE FOR

When Wolves Become Birds

"Lovely imagery, driven by real passion."

— Francesca Lia Block

"Poems which are full of evocative phrases (*the gnarled fingers of crones, a birch bark church*) and beautiful images (*an eclipse of moths, in spring I molt winter's wings*)."

— Yuka Igarashi

"Poems [that] are savage yet vulnerable, [with] breathtaking twists of language: talons in the earth and wings soaring in the sky. Transcendent imagery, deep-diving beneath the pelt of women to the beating heart, and the fiery brain. I was spellbound."

— David Henry Sterry

When Wolves Become Birds

When
Wolves

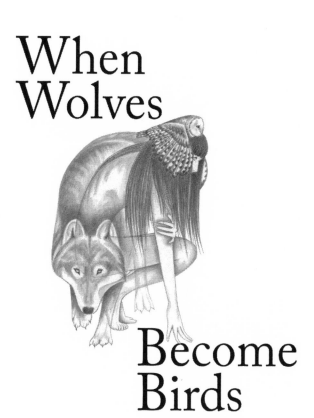

Become
Birds

ALISE VERSELLA

2021
GOLDEN DRAGONFLY PRESS

FIRST PRINT EDITION, February 2021
FIRST EBOOK EDITION, February 2021

Cover Illustration by Andrea Hrnjak.
Copyright © 2021 by Alise Versella.

ISBN–13: 978-1-7330099-4-2

Library of Congress Control Number: 2020952364

Printed on acid-free paper supplied by a
Forest Stewardship Council-certified provider.
First published in the United States of America
by Golden Dragonfly Press, 2021.

www.goldendragonflypress.com

www.aliseversella.com

This is for the wolf girls

Contents

I Have Never Written Love Poems

Never felt they gut me
The way a hunter guts his kill

      You need to cut open the body
      Disembowel it
      Before the innards poison the meat

You are holding onto heartbreak
Because it produces better poetry

The trick of it is never write a poem
To live flesh

Write instead to what has passed

One day you will look upon the bloodstained forest
Not with regret

You will thank the deer for its sustenance
And the hunter the strong stomach needed
To empty
You
Out

Hunting Season

The only stars I see leave tracks in mud
　　　　animal eyes glowing in the moonlight

My words have become
Incantations in the dark
Like an owl squawking on his branch
They perch upon my tongue

Wet leaves twist through claws of wind
My shutter lungs torn open
No sweet reprieve for Artemis
Huntress, banshee queen

The moon watches the mirrored
Riverbank ripple with rumbling hooves
A stag sheds his velvet horns
And the rain-soaked mountains mourn

The Girl I Thought I Was

I bargained my soul
Watched it leave my body
Through a pyramid of quartz

I was looking for my shadow
In blood-red moonlight
My reflection in sleeting rain

My voice was a hollow howl
Echoing
        Then fading

All I could offer was my pain
Carved from these seven layers of flesh
So I gave the scorned king
The marrow from my bones
In exchange
For a burial in snow
The pine trees shriveled
Like the gnarled fingers of crones

The crows made a bed for me from their feathers
        A nest for my corpse

And I succumbed to the dying
Surrendered to the frost
To grieve the girl I thought I was.

The Morrigan

I've drowned to breathe
Become the salt of the sea
While the desert lies parched with its thirst
The earth will crack
Swallow me up

Would that be considered triumph?

I hear the drums of battle pounding
Like the thunder pounds in my chest
Every time I open my mouth
The scream of crows
Comes out instead

The vultures lie in wait
To make
A nest of my bleached-white bones
Drying in the sun

If I sacrifice the marrow
What do I become?

This Is How We Change

September is for the golden leaves
October for the dead ones
November turns their skeleton
Stems to ash
December is the tomb
        That holds the birch box casket
        Below six inches of snow
        No headstone

I can smell the decay of October
Like you smell the roses in May
Only I hear the owls
        Hollow
        And the crows
While you whistle a tune
Knife sharp
Like your favorite jays

They attack other birds you know
Brutishly they dive
Naivety would have you compare them to mothers
   who protect their young
But I say it's downright similar to greedy men
Securing their wealth- attractive bantam birds,
   guarding their plethora of worms

A warble becomes a shriek
Tiny feet-
Talons clawing into feathers that will become

strangled and bent
So you will never fly right again

This is how seasons change.
How our fortunes are divined through a wind gust
of tea leaves
We are never more ourselves than in a candid moment

The afternoon sun will set the leaves to burn
Like a kiln sets fire to wet clay
Harden and temper the perceptions we create
As we brace ourselves for the cold and the snow
    and the dark

Await the obvious black-tipped blue
The plucked-out casualty
So jarring against
Soundless white

Grave Robbing

The bone yard by the sea is where he drowned me
My teeth are cold where I bit my cheek
Holding coins for Hades underneath my tongue
Fox-tails comforted me up 'til now
But in the woods the crows hold their vigil, still
Each shriek and their feathers fly
Out of cavernous eyes
In calcified
Skulls
Dug
From the mausoleum
The ghost of a full moon rises
And sonar waves violently
Spread out a route
For all the bats
Owl talons shred the ground
Ripping up the pieces of
Eurydice's broken crown
The morning glory sings of Orpheus
In an opiate haze he fades
In and out
A ghost whistling as he haunts

The nightshade and the hemlock

A Hallowed Space

Hold a space for me
Between
The darkened winter leaves
Breathe the frost
Clinging to frozen oaks

Bury my bones in the dirt
The hallowed ground of a birch bark church

I have fought wars with echoes
In small ponds
Drowning the whippoorwill
Until
Juniper berries stained the shadows

"I am [still] half sick of shadows"

Bury my hunter's heart in the forest
Where my ghosts and cold snow
Are laden heavily on the
Evergreen branches
My soul is an eclipse of moths
Reduced to soot and ashes
Burning in a bleeding Borealis

45 Applebe Avenue

I sat on a bench
Under a fig tree
When I was four
And by an owl I was blessed

That feather made of me
Something dark and deep
Unruly like the sky or the sea
All these years

And I still feel trapped inside this covering
Fighting wars with bone and flesh

One Day I Will Go through Menopause and I Won't Sweat a Breakup

I shouldn't have to bleed
For the things I think are owed to me

Like selfless love
After all these years of giving
Did I not give enough of my blood?

Every month
How I thanked some god above
For the chemistry
I swallowed

Don't you love how I don't spit I swallow?
And I swallowed every word
And I believed you

Believed mine was the love that freed you
While tirelessly building a pen to corral myself into

I don't need to need you
But I wanted to

Why wasn't that enough for you?

Loving you shouldn't mean loving myself less
Like I am some creature the hunter can possess
Look at the rabbit heart I pulled beating from its chest
But I am no rabbit running
I am the bear

And it is not fair
To roll over now and play dead
Like I didn't use the last of my arrows to defend you

The bow was made from willow trees
But this body was not made for bending

The birds are aware of love's ending
Before the heart knows
They alight from the branches like when a storm comes

They don't have the language to say
What broken hearts become

But if I keep bleeding will time tell?

The Owl Tattoo

Spread it out
Against the curve of my hip
Partially hidden
Just below the lace trim
An explosion of fierce feathers
Thrashing against bone

I am Hecate, the dark crone
I have flown
From the shadows to be shaded
Like stitches of an old scar, sewn
Pin these wings in flight
So they wrap around me tightly
Clutching the thin skin
With the blood-blue veins
Fill them in with ink

Trace my heart with black lines
I want to see my soul made visceral
I want to see the talons tearing at my onion heart
Until
It seizes

Draw me the depths of its bleeding
And when the needle has finished
Its abuse of skin
I want to find a new me underneath it

Cloisonné Vase

I have been molded
From hardened and tempered clay

And I cry for all the
Fissures
Beginning to crack
Inside of me

Lilly

Make me like creation
In the start of Genesis
Crashing light
And green
And fire
Roiling tides and raging seas
The biblical recount of my release

Strip me of my flesh and bone
So from my shoulder blades have sprung
The wings of which the feathers fall
To show from where I've flown

Make me like a revelation
Rechristen me
In the fires of my suffering
So I may find new meaning
In my sins

Make my lungs sing gospels from the psalms
Make me like a hymn
Forged like steel
Torn from Adam's rib

Fern Hollow

I am made of bone
             And feather
              And fur
My skull is home to crows
I shift shape in the snow
In spring I molt winter's wings
Beneath these quills my heart beats
My forests grow wild and free
With butterflies and stinging bees
I am Eden's tree
My ribcage blooms with marigolds and daisies
Owls make nocturnal nests
In between my shoulder blades
I dance like a few wild stanzas
Tribal dancing
            Pounding
My talons into the mud
Until all my feathers will fall out
Until I finally come undone

Winter Hush

I crave to inhale the poisoned scent
Of dying winter blooms
One last attempt
For this quiescent tree to breed
Its saccharine fruit

But winter is not meant for decomposing things
October's wet dead leaves
        Their premonitions of death

The darkened winter in its latency
Allows the shedding
A rebirth
        A transformation
And I will alight with sparrows come the thaw of spring

Crow Totem

This soft, human flesh
Proves insufficient covering
Belies the strength of muscled mass
Attached to ligaments inside of me
The homo-sapien taxonomy
Wasted on these weak stemmed vertebrae
I much prefer the coarse tongued beauty
Of burning haunches, taut
Swiftly cutting through my dark
I lust shifting bones
That crack inside their sockets
To break and reconnect,
Fuse together like the stitched seams of a pocket
I crave to tear at these old, dry veins
With the talons of some bird of prey
Reflecting the moon as it pulls these menstrual tides
and orchestrate the stale heart to commence its symphony
Oh! The animal blood and its glorious singing
My lungs let loose a wild cry
I am the dark crow
Warning
The imminence of my transitioning

The Phoenix

I laid my heart in the sepulcher for its martyrdom
Left all my entrails for the vultures to feast upon
They can have the flesh mass of me
All the meat of the brain and its vapidity
I need not the caverns of this carcass any more
The pharaohs lie in their sarcophagi
Emptied of their insides
Why not I?

This witch has been sent to burn
But I prefer to catch fire freely
Shake loose these ropes
Tied around my throat
To prevent my tongue from slipping
Out passed the walls of my feral teeth
So the howl won't cast its spell
Weaved from my banshee mouth

Like Joan of Arc
I've relinquished my heart
Ripped it out
        Bloodied

Like my feathered parts
To rise from the flames of their pyres
        Rebirthed
Because I am mythic
And unafraid to
Burn

I Used to Be Tame Once

I used to sing
About the unwinding of a hot summer evening
The crash of our souls upon the body of the beach
And now my heart is unbinding
As the salt slams up against the jetty rocks
          I sing now

About the culmination of a season releasing its demons
How man becomes the lion
          And the lion becomes a beast
Ensnares the gazelle in his pointed teeth

The water's rushing in and we're submerged in the tide
Drowning in the voices
Of ghosts

Then the voice sings out!
          It echoes
Through the sunken halls of shipwrecked lungs
Panics the heart that couldn't recognize
The beat of its own song
          That ghost in the throat is my own

I will sing of oceans tumbling
Of the untamed Serengeti
          The wild beast inside of me
An ocean will spill like ink from out of me
The words clawing their way out
Growling

I will never be tame

Seeds Do Not Shrink Smaller
into the Soil, They Unfurl

See how the petals bleed when crushed between
    my thumbs?
Like so many throats crushed by the weight of
    someone else's words on the tongue
That a stem could be so fragile and yet turn into an oak
The same way spells are made stronger by the
    words invoked

Leaves can't help but rustle through a breeze
Still I prune my tallest branches, fear the splintered
broken bark
That would interfere with the wires electricity
    would traverse
So afraid of storms that could uproot me and
lightning's splitting spark

I am so surprised by how birds fly through the
    ever-changing night
Taken aback by how their white wings never
disappear into the ink
I've lost faith in how a fading pulse can be pulled
    back from the brink
How a voice can return as an echo down an empty street

We are never really lost you see we just transform
The way nectar becomes honey by bees fanning
their comb

Why do I swallow split sentences down a swollen throat?
Lose these shackles from strained vocal cords
There is a garden escaping through the ribcage that
houses these lungs

All Demi-Gods Sing Off-Key

I've ceased shaving
At least this way
Perhaps
I can slowly change into a Minotaur
Boys tell me I am some mythic monster
Anyhow
A beast the sons of gods are sent to slaughter

Like they are Hera
Forever threatened by
My beauty and my power

But I am not beautiful
I am like a harpy
And I've carved out all the hearts
Of all the men
Who've caused my heart to break

I am Eurydice who steps on the snake
Whose arms always slither around my waist
When I try to dance by myself

They tell me I sing off–key
Fuck them
Because I still love to sing

Perhaps the beast is only trapped in a labyrinth
Because her captors are afraid
Of their own wild; hiding
Too ashamed to admit it is the same

Like Diana, of the hunt with her werewolves
Running rampant with their dark selves
Free of mortal shackles
Ferocity unleashed by moonlight
As my bloated belly swells

And they are afraid of my blood
Like it will crash over the shore and drown them
But I am made white bone
And silk milk skin
By the moon that reigns these tides in
My shadows may swell
But my blood while it pumps through my veins
Sings triumphant from my lungs

Where Does Self-Doubt Measure on the Richter Scale?

I have divided my body like the world halved by
    an equator
Each part of me a city built among a fault line

Here comes the tremor

Sending a frenzy of birds to take flight from
    my branches

But I will send these streets to fire first
Light them up like sage

And I will become the moon to control the tides

Notice how the ocean waves don't ever look behind
At the horizon

They just keep breaking forward towards the shore

So I may be the earth quaking
               Crumbling

But I will never doubt the strength of my core

The State of Burning

The pounding wings of vultures
Fly around inside my lungs
Feeding on all the dead things
I was choking on

The heart that I've kept hidden
Is ready now to bleed
Freely; pomegranate red
Like the flames
Devouring the leaves

Casting shadows of the winter pines, those
    skeleton trees
My soul breaks free from the bark frame cage

The most potent of spells
Are cast by the tongue
They alkalize in the tunnels of these lungs

I am wild like a fire
That will not be controlled
Laying waste the dormant ground as I grow

Catharsis comes from fire the louder I roar
Sparks catch
Every time my lips strike match

Deposits in the Dirt

I came upon a small dark wood
The ferns were trembling
The bees had laid their weapons down
The flora ceased breathing

I could not tell you how
All the birds shook loose their feathers
And the trees their leaves from the boughs

But I think it's the roots of things
That digs into the marrow
And terrify these weeds
They know now I'm not afraid to say aloud
The things I truly mean

Lanoka Harbor

I live in a town of harbors and boats
Where I've built my sterns from pinecones
My sails sap stained from evergreens
And pine needles have anchored my feet

This heart is a soft blue crab shell
Hiding in the sand of brackish lagoons
Seaweed has tangled through my veins
My blood and the lake share the same hue

My lips stained by cranberries
My lungs fill up with stars
My feet dash passed lithe deer
Pounding their hooves in the dark

I run and I breathe in the pine and the scent
Of honeysuckle and wait
By the dock on the bay for the horizon line
To shimmer gold over the sea

I wait for the sun to shine over me
For the salt to wash me clean
To smooth the jagged parts
Like abalone 'til I gleam

I Stand at the Shoreline, Captain

I smell the salt first
But it is not the same scent
As my sweat or   the water to boil the linguine
                              or salt I swill to heal my
bleeding gums
It is the sweet inhale
The babe whose finished teething   the muscles
                  releasing the tension they've held

That these waves turquoise and green
Could be
The plunder
                  The toil
                  And the drowning
Still the
                  Safety
                  Sweet kiss of seaweed
                  Holding
Home
That the higher they crest and the   farther they pull
I stay firmly planted. Roots.
The gulls go after crabs and the crabs go after my toes

Oh sand between the toes it has been too long
            Like an old friend you've been away too long
This is like returning where I've always belonged
            Though back then it always felt forced

But the sunlight on this coast
Has always been mine
        That gold and traffic light
        Street's amber glow and brake light
        B l I n k I n g like my heart

I draw maps in the sand like lines on my palm
All these points lead back...

Shore is home

When we are famished like teen girls in love
Our anorexia-survival
Seeking to make ourselves full of something more

Don't you remember, teen girl
Just wants the world to love her back

Home will remind her she has an ocean for a stomach
Her hurricane waves will hungrily
Devour the dock

I will let an ocean enter me
Because I need the sting of the sea

To remind me how to breathe
To remind me of the ocean I hold between my legs.

I Will Never Say I Need You

If only I didn't want too much
If only I settled for just good enough
But mediocrity
Was never for me
I believe
I want it all
You see I don't just want you to bring me down the moon
I want the whole fucking universe
In fact, forget you
I can grab it myself
Been working on these biceps
So I don't need to
Need you

If only I wasn't so selfish
Didn't put my foot down first
So timid
Like I didn't
Actually deserve to walk
High and mighty
Upon this earth

You see I already learned about self-worth

I am not ashamed of my flaws
Because
It has taken me too long to love these scars

I am nothing less than a "phenomenal woman
Phenomenally"

A glorious human being
And I love myself
And all my wild paradox

How I want everything in its proper place
But there are holes in all my socks

I never said I wasn't difficult

Loving
Loving is difficult

But I am not so easily
The kind of girl
Who gives up what she wants

Diana, the Huntress

The horned woman resides in the forest beside the
bark king

But the pelted beasts run not as fast as she

The feathered ones get lost in the expanse of her wings
The river ripples under the quake of her feet
The wind sighs through the grass

And night crawlers bask
        in her looming shadow
Hunters cannot tame her arrows
She is the mounted skull you'll never possess

No, my heart you will never possess
        never will you reach close enough to
           pierce this flesh

She pledges loyalty only to the earth
The girl is queen
        sovereign to herself

I Don't Care to Be Pretty

I will never be the girl with the pretty mouth
For the girl with the pretty mouth is the girl
Who will eventually get slapped
Along the length of it

Who will grow ashamed
Of its curling corners
Because everyone will tell her to smile
Show teeth

Well here are my teeth and molars biting
And I do not have a sweet
Tongue

I am always just a little bit bothersome
My words and opinions
Grating like mosquitos
Sucking and draining

I will draw your blood

I will leave an impression
You might not like

But I will leave one

Like the indentations bodies make in grass
Bloody and
Outlined by chalk

The entry mark
A blemish
Like acne on my skin

I refuse to cover up

Witness my ugly
My grime and filth
Like the sewers in the city
This is my humanity
The sick of me

You don't deserve what thrives in this garden
If you cannot come to terms with worms
The maggots that will make a home
Of my rotting flesh
You don't deserve my best

I don't trade pleasantries with hypocrites
Misogynists

I am not the girl with the pretty mouth
My mouth is a dark cavern
Gaping like the hole Munch painted

A mirror to reflect your vulgarity
So do not tell me
I don't sound like a lady

What makes you think you sound like a man?

In Defense of My Existence

Philomela was raped
And before she could bring
A kingdom to his knees
King Tereus cut out her tongue

> They wish they could sever a tongue from
> this hellish mouth

The gods turned her into a nightingale
Like somehow flight would save her

> Not like every time young girls first learn
> to fly
> Learn the broad range of their wings and
> the length of their shadow
> Only to have those great wings bound
> Oh how

I've had enough of someone pinning my wings down

In nature the only sound
Of the nightingale
Comes from the mouth of the male
The gods did Philomela no favor

> You must learn as a woman to become
> your own savior

Philomela's sister served King Tereus his own son
On a platter
Penance for the wrong he'd done

We will serve you your future sons on a
    platter with our blood
For we deserve a future better than the seeds
    you've sown
And I will not sink silently into the mud
I will not go quietly
You won't drown out this voice in a flood
Every time a hawk screams or a crow

Or a banshee on your war fields
Know
Every splitting fiber in the marrow of your bones
Was felt by a woman first
You will no longer bury our severed tongues in the dirt

Philomela will not be reduced to myth
She will stand testament
To history
Until a new story
Takes precedence

A Girl's Whole Life Can Be Found in Her Purse

She empties her purse
Like the galaxy empties its milky way over the desert
The contents spill out
Like the hopeful prayers of teen girls who still
believe god travels via shooting star

She empties her purse

And tosses the Revlon red in the trash because that's
    how he made her feel when she wore it
Her mouth a pretty stain like the stain on the carpet
"Why did we ever wear blue-white eye shadow?"
Like somehow it made us more adult to wear such
unflattering makeup
"What's this infatuation with girls and their makeup?"
She throws that too in the trash and mumbles, "Fuck it."
As if the absence of color on her face would stop
them from staring

It doesn't

She cuts the credit card in half
The one she charged for the cab to take her home
The one with higher limits than the levels of booze
in his blood
"My mother always told me to keep extra money for
    a ride"
Like god forbid anyone act dignified

Before trying to get between our thighs
The plastic cracks like the makeup she slept in

"I should invest in waterproof mascara because it
always runs when I cry"

"Men name their cars so I named my purse. I call
her Priscilla.
Not like his wife.
More like queen of the desert."

She empties her purse

But keeps the license
Not merely a privilege awarded, but more like that
freedom we sought

"We keep trying to fill ourselves up
 Like we are not already enough,
I think I'll just keep on driving, ride these roads
into the desert and find something
Altogether different to fill the contents of my purse with."

She didn't want to be queen of just the desert; she
wanted to be queen of herself

You can tell a lot about a girl by what she keeps in
her purse
It's like we keep our whole life there
To carry it close
And it weighs some of us down like a burden or a curse

No wonder she dumped it all out
She'd rather carry the universe
In her heart

Where it counts

Dangerous and Noble Things

My head is a flock of great winged birds
Beating their escape from the pressures of their cages
For the raw freedom
Atop winter's sparse tree branches

I will coat these frozen limbs
With the down of soft snow feathers
And prove to violet spring
That these branches can carry the weight

I am on the cusp of an awakening
As the snow hangs
Heavy
In the belly of the clouds
Ready to birth its storm
From the firmament

And I will fly to greet the frost that forms
Ice on my eyelashes
I will be that great snow owl
Finding strength in whitewashed fields
That blind in glaring winter sun
Forcing our eyes to see
All we'd rather disregard
The white lies we tell ourselves
The way we keep our great wings bound

Mine are sprawled out once more
I had forgotten the broad range of their shadow
How powerful and strong

Like these evergreen trees and their command of
the snow

And it is in the hush of falling snow that surrounds me
Like a great winged bird atop the tallest evergreen
In a snow-covered forest
I have found autonomy

A Natural Disaster

They say my blood is tainted
It's in my DNA
Like the ground beneath me
How the core boils
The earth quaking

They say I erupt
Like the volcano
My rage flows from my veins
Like the lava in Kilauea reclaiming its space

It is okay to want to reclaim your space

I've held out like rain in drought for too long
Been holding my breath in my lungs for too long
I will not stay quiet any longer
Breath exhaled and the shingles tear from the roof

The wind whips up a gale on the horizon
The Santa Ana's always set the highways on fire

I have singed my throat with soot and ash
My eyes are the lightning
The electric cracking through your birch bark bones

So much pain
And the rain is only welcome when the earth is thirsty?

It is okay to cry here

I will not drown in the ground turned to mud and mulch
No, I am not too much

The people want to flee from me
Afraid of what they see in me

They could never cause the tides to rise
Shake the fault lines
Fray the power lines

They beg me, "Tamp down your flaws"
Blind to the exquisiteness in every natural disaster
Like the princess cannot be both reprieve and hazard

And still get her happily ever after

After every natural disaster nature sets herself free
The wolf becomes a bird
Her wings released

The Distance between Two Selves

Consider the distance between two points
The first is a height
The second the fear of the climb
And the distance extends out like a telescope
The farther a star moves away
It's in this way
Wings betray a blue jay

But consider the altitudes a body can reach
Like a body asleep projects the soul to an astral plane
How a dream
Given branches, builds a nest
A home
And does not second guess
Feathers
Left to compost

Heavy may be the bags of bitter salt
That break open like the earth
Or the heart
Heavy handed it spreads
Like chaos
The load trusted more than the ability to bear it

The lover, considered foolish
How she lets her body burst forth
With brilliant understanding
Of what it means to love someone as much as she
loves herself

Stop trying to calculate what can't be measured
Like ocean fathoms
And familiar phantoms
Their hauntings mistaken for friendship

Trust again in the night sky
Do not mourn the fading of its stars as they burn
Scorching the arid dirt
You are the sapling reaching, but you are not the
binding root
And your tears will not set the ground aflame
They extinguish the thirst
Of so many choking doves

Darling the mountain is never the obstacle
It has always been your fear of the stumble
Do you think all fledging birds
Consider
Distance
Before they learn
Flight
No
They simply fly

If Planted, Flowers Will Grow
in a Bone Yard

This good dirt
Is good enough
For the oranges and the persimmons
The roses
And the marigolds
The oleander and the tuberose
The bougainvillea only grows
As the oak tree roots burrow
Deeper
Into this good dirt
Which was good enough for Whitman
And this compost
So I think this plot of soil
Will be suitable for me
The dry brittle bones and me
Will sink into this earth six feet
And out of the planted seeds of me
A garden will grow for you
And you shall see what I see
That the world has never been against you

I Am Here for Me

Do not be enslaved
By your own derisive thoughts
By time trapped in its clocks
By what the world believes you should have achieved
At what age and what you should
Want

You
Have no one else to answer to but yourself
Do not let this beautifully cruel world make you feel
small
Do not let anyone
Make you feel insignificant
You are a tapestry of woven stars
And you are infinite

When Wolves Become Birds

Growing: snapping bones, tight skin

What shall become of werewolf girls
Who shave their pelts and molt
Feathers instead
Who, at full moons, seek out the stars
With their wings?

What happens when you finally believe
You are worthy of life below this vast sky
And that this sky is yours?

It's hers and his and ours
The hours are counting down
And I like the sound of endless possibility
I like the sound of my heartbeats at midnight

Wolves become birds and we'll fly
Our howls becoming songs
Mockingbirds repeat

I Will Edit Manuscripts,
but I Will Not Edit Myself

I do not wish for snapshots
I want the whole damn panorama
I want the extended cut
The unedited scroll
You let roll forth from the typewriter

Like a carpet you did not have pulled out from under you
And I want the dust you swept under that carpet
When your mother wasn't looking
When you were tired of the nagging

After you unpacked all the boxes of your body you
    kept closed up
Taped shut
Because you have been so afraid to unpack your baggage
And buy furniture with sturdy legs
Legs that will dent the carpet
Legs that might scratch that hardwood if you don't
first lay down some velvet to buffer it

I say refuse all buffers
Like bowling without bumpers
Like I do not care if sometimes my ball lies in the gutter

Scream guttural if you cracked the mirror and today
    didn't like the imperfect reflection
Scream if it makes you feel better
because hawks don't consider the eardrums of earthworms
they scream because they're flying high and hunting

They are taking all that opportunity has laid before them
Because God gave them claws
So do not retract yours

We have deemed declawing inhumane
So what if you scratch a little?
If you sting a little
If the blood reminds the spineless
You are still here?

For All the Dreams
I Still Have Yet to Dream
and All the Dreams Once Had

I said I wanna cast spells mother
Let the pearls drip forth from the oyster shell of my mouth
I wanna
Taste the cities mother
Hold the earth like a lover holds my hips above the
ledge of his

I won't hold secrets and empty promises
I want blood oath and lightning strikes, terror and
the shriek of a nightmare
Jolting me alive
Nocturnal birds once the day sets

Watch the girls as they set their masks down
Embrace our dark nights and vulnerability
That I still cry
And shout so you can hear me
Over the sting in my throat
The sting of this salt
These cresting waves
I swear to god one day I'm gonna drown in

But for now
I'm learning how to float
How to sip of love and not get drunk
Oh! How the tide wants to pull me back with her
But I am still a stubborn woman, mother

I am learning how to take a fighter's stance
On shifting plates, I try to pirouette
And I am graceless

But thank god for that
thank god for my vulgar mouth and my too small
hands
They hold this bleeding organ like an offering
To no god at all but my younger self
That holy ghost
haunting skeletal halls that creak a little more upon
waking now

Kneecaps remember what it was like to run
Hunched
Howling
Because it hurt to learn I must become a beast

Some of us never shed the pelt for wings
Forget we were made for skies
And we make our own heavens from the pearly gates
of our teeth

A smile that bites back
Like a dog in the junkyard
A warning behind a chain link fence

We were all born in the gutter with our eyes full of stars
Mother
Maybe we did fall to earth from mars
But I still believe in what we've been building here
Even if we burn it down daily
Aren't we all witches set to burn at the stake daily?
Joan of Arc and maybe I am crazy

Crazy as my feet levitate from the grass as I dance
and spin
Righteous, divine like a dervish
I spin in the grass and the dew wets my cheeks
    I think I'm crying

For all the lost souls who once held mad dreams
Foaming like the seashore at the mouth of their bays

There is no jetty jagged enough to break my wake
Oh, I am dreaming mother do not attempt to
    wake me...

A Walking Verse of Poetry

Look how far you've come
How glorious you've become
How much lighter and free
How strong
Self-assured
God damn girl how good it feels to love your fucking self

To have gone after your dreams
Look at all you have achieved

This body. This walking verse of poetry.

How delicious it all tastes now that I no longer hold
    my tongue

Watch me
The wolf girl shedding a coarse pelt
Watch me soar like a hawk
It feels so good to dig these talons through the dirt
Fuck it all up. The grave they tried to dig for me...
I made an Eden of it.

Acknowledgments

Do YOU KNOW how long it takes before a fledgling Great Horned Owl can fly from its nest? According to the Audubon Society, 9–10 weeks. The Broad-Winged Hawk takes 5–6.

Do you know how long it took a wolf girl to reclaim her wings? 6 years. For the last six years, I have prowled the floor of the forests searching for a nest to hold me. I have finally found that nest. Golden Dragonfly Press has given me a home and I couldn't be more proud to be part of its long list of talented writers. Alice, I am eternally grateful to you.

Thank you to David Henry Sterry and Arielle Eckstut for their expertise and belief in this manuscript and my poetry in general. To David especially for his edits on this manuscript and the effort put forth into helping me find it a home.

Francesca Lia Block for being my inspiration from an early age, my teacher and a trusted advisor in every form this manuscript took, thank you for helping shape these poems. Thank you for helping shape me.

My New Jersey poetry community: Chris Rockwell, Kelso A. Nickels, AK Hanrahan, Chelsea Palermo, Mychal Mills, Brave New Words, to name just a few among the many. You have invited me in and nurtured me, giving me the strength to venture from a nest in the first place. That my voice sings out now is because of you.

To my online community: *Rebelle Society* and *Women's Spiritual Poetry* especially. Soumyajeet Chattaraj and Catherine Schweig I cannot thank you enough for the doors you have opened for me.

To my family and friends who have consistently re-minded me of my wolf strength and the broad shadow of my wings, for applauding at every open mic and read-ing every first draft, thank you, I love you.

The utmost gratitude to the editors of the journals where these poems first appeared:

"This is how we Change", "Crow Totem", and "Dangerous and Noble Things" previously published on *Entropy* as part of their #thebirds series

"Grave Robbing" previously published in issue 16 of *Three Drops from a Cauldron*

"A Hallowed Space" previously published on *Ultraviolet Tribe*

"Fern Hollow" previously published on *Grimoire Noir*

"Diana, The Huntress" previously published in *Goddess: When She Rules — Expressions by Contemporary Women* Anthology

"I Don't Care to be Pretty", and "In Defense of my Existence" previously published on *What Rough Beast* by Indolent Books

"I Am Here for Me," and "If Planted, Flowers Will Grow in a Bone Yard" previously published in *The Opi-ate Magazine*

"The Distance between Two Selves," and "I Will Edit Manuscripts, but I Will Not Edit Myself" previously published in *COG Magazine*

Other Books by Alise

Five Foot Voice: The Selected Works of Alise Versella

Onion Heart: Peel Back Your Layers

A Few Wild Stanzas: Poems

Made in the USA
Middletown, DE
06 December 2021